On Christmas Night

Bob Chilcott

for upper voices, SATB, and organ or chamber ensemble

Contents

Suggested readings are given at the relevant points in the score.

MUSIC DEPARTMENT

OXFORD
UNIVERSITY PRESS

Composer's note

On Christmas Night is made up of eight carol settings that follow the sequence of the Christmas story—from the fall of Adam, through the promise of a child's coming and the journey of Mary and Joseph to Bethlehem, to the birth of the baby Jesus. I have designed the piece to be as flexible as possible in terms of performance. It can be sung either liturgically or in concert, including the suggested readings or any other similar readings of choice. The piece can also be performed without readings, or individual carols can be sung separately. I have incorporated several traditional carols, both texts and melodies (the latter occasionally slightly altered), and these feature most often in the upper-voice part. This part can be sung by a children's choir, by a small group of sopranos from the SATB choir, or even, if felt appropriate, by the audience or congregation. The musical performance could also be complemented by dancers, as was the case at the work's premiere at University Christian Church in Austin, Texas.

Duration: *c*.23 minutes (without readings)

An accompaniment for chamber ensemble (fl, ob, perc, hp, org) is available on hire/rental from the publisher or appropriate agent. For ensemble performances, the organ part available on hire/rental should be used, rather than the part in the vocal score.

OXFORD
UNIVERSITY PRESS

Great Clarendon Street, Oxford OX2 6DP, England

Oxford is a registered trade mark of Oxford University Press in the UK and in certain other countries

© Oxford University Press 2011

Bob Chilcott has asserted his right under the Copyright, Designs and Patents Act, 1988,
to be identified as the Composer of this Work

Database right Oxford University Press (maker)

First published 2011

ISBN 978–0–19–337560–4

Music and text origination by Enigma Music Production Services, Amersham, Bucks
Printed in Great Britain on acid-free paper by Halstan & Co. Ltd, Amersham, Bucks

*Commissioned by University Christian Church, Austin, Texas,
in memory of Dr Lawrence W. Bash through a bequest made by Roy Cates*

On Christmas Night

1. This is the truth (I)

Trad. English

BOB CHILCOTT

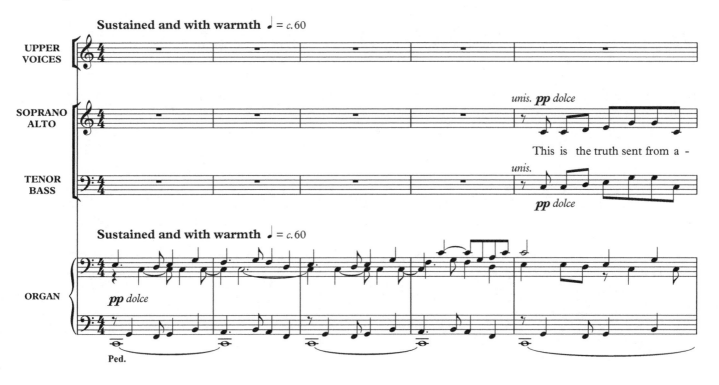

First performed on 12 December 2010 at University Christian Church, Austin, Texas, conducted by Bob Chilcott.

4

*Melody by Henry John Gauntlett (1805–76); text by Mrs Cecil Frances Alexander (1818–95)

24

mf

Ma - ry was that mo - ther mild, Je - sus Christ her lit - tle child.

next thing which to you I tell, Wo-man was made with him to dwell.

mf

Man.

28

p *cresc.*

Thus we were heirs to

unis. **p** *cresc.*

Thus we were heirs to end-less woes Till

unis.

p *cresc.*

p *cresc.*

Ped.

Suggested Reading 1: Genesis 3: 8–15

2. Adam lay ybounden

15th cent.

BOB CHILCOTT

Light and mobile ♩ = *c.*144

SOPRANO
ALTO

TENOR
BASS

Light and mobile ♩ = *c.*144

ORGAN

p

Man.

A - dam lay__ y-bound-en,_____ Bound-en in__ a bond;_____

Four thou - sand win - ter_____ Thought he not_____ too long._____

And all was for an ap - ple,

An ap - ple that he took,_____ As clerk - es[1] find - en_____

Ne had the ap - ple

_____ Writ - ten in_____ their book.[2]

ta - ken been,_____ The ap - ple_____ ta - ken been,_____

[1] clergy
[2] the Bible

ap - ple ta - ken was;_____ There-fore we__moun[3] sing - en:____

'De - o gra - ci - as!____ De - o gra - ci - as!____

De - o gra - ci - as!'_____

[3]must

Suggested Reading 2: Isaiah 9: 2, 6–7

3. A spotless Rose

14th-cent. German
trans. Catherine Winkworth (1827–78)

BOB CHILCOTT

*Melody 14th-cent. German; text trans. Theodore Baker (1851–1934)

Suggested Reading 3: Luke 1: 26–35, 38

4. The Cherry Tree Carol

Trad. English

BOB CHILCOTT

18

Suggested Reading 4: Luke 2: 1, 3–7

5. O little town

Phillips Brooks (1835–93) **BOB CHILCOTT**

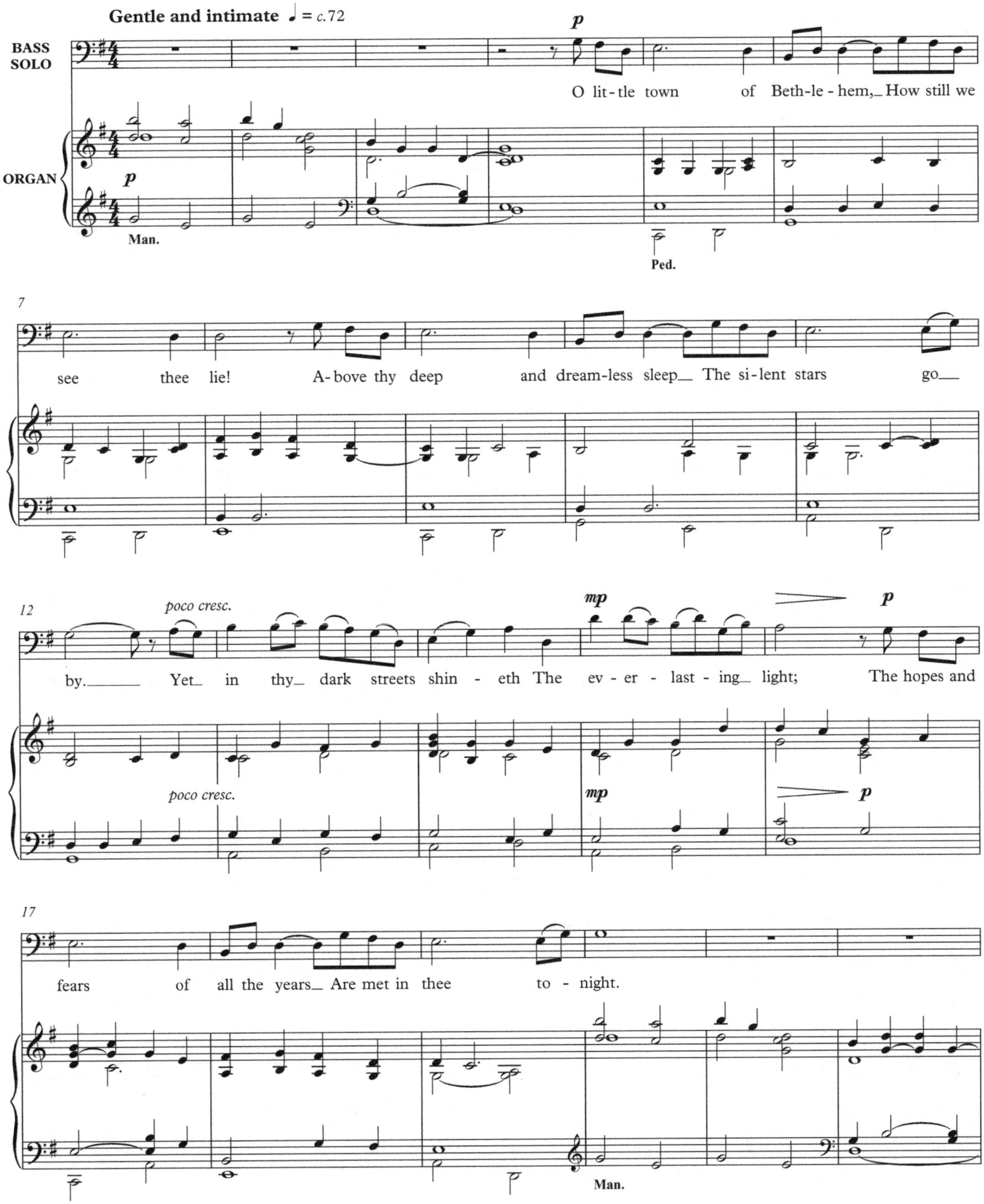

*The alto solo part may alternatively be sung by upper voices.
†Melody: Trad. English

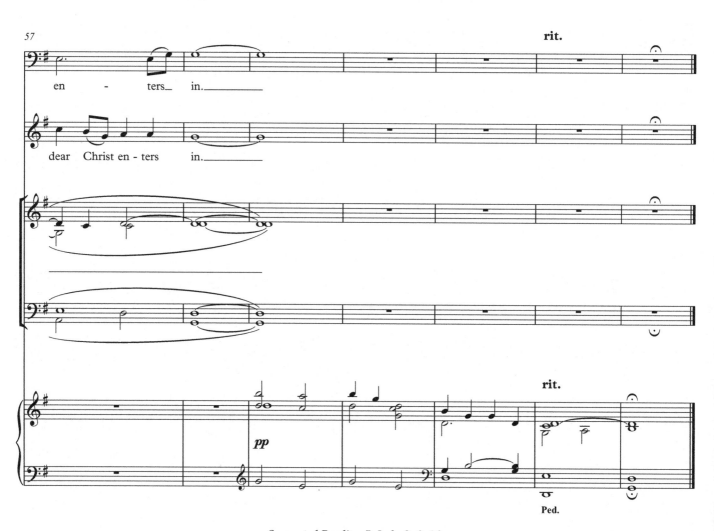

52

com-ing; But in this world of sin, Where meek souls will re-ceive him, still The dear Christ

com-ing; But in this world of sin, Where meek souls will re-ceive him, still The

com-ing; But in this world of sin, oo

hear, in this world of sin,

57

en-ters in.

dear Christ en-ters in.

rit.

rit.

pp

Ped.

Suggested Reading 5: Luke 2: 8–16

6. Sweet was the song

from William Ballet's Lute Book (16th cent.)

BOB CHILCOTT

[1] pronounce as in 'lullaby' and not *loo-la*

*The soprano solo part may alternatively be sung by upper voices.

26

(TUTTI)

S.
A.

'Sweet babe, sweet babe', sang she, 'My son, And

T.
B.

eke² a Sa - viour born, Who has vouch - safed³ from on high To

vi - sit us that were for - lorn.' La - lul - la, la - lul - la, la - lul - la-

la - lul - la-

la - lul - la-

² also
³ granted

*Melody by Franz Xaver Gruber (1787–1863); original German text by Joseph Mohr (1792–1848), trans. John F. Young (1820–85)

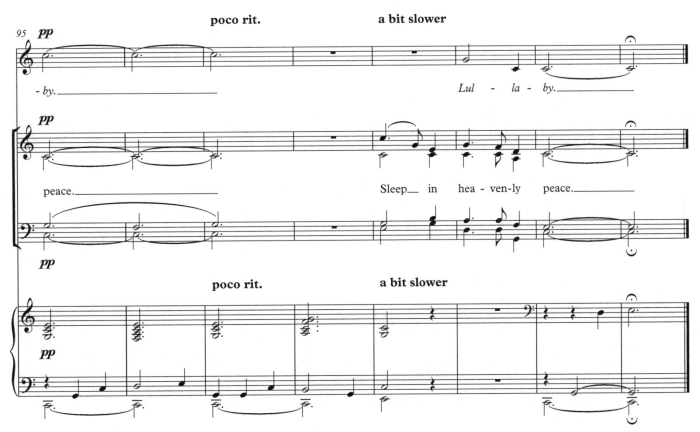

Suggested Reading 6: Matthew 2: 1–11

7. Rejoice and be merry

Trad. English

BOB CHILCOTT

mor - tals on earth! For this is the birth-day of Je - sus our King, Who brought us sal-

-va - tion: his prai - ses we'll sing!

Re-joice, re - joice, re-joice, re - joice!

Re - joice, re-joice, re - joice, re - joice!

A hea - ven - ly vi - sion ap - peared in the sky;— Vast num - bers of

an - gels the shep - herds did spy, Pro - claim - ing the birth - day of Je - sus our

King, Who brought us sal - va - tion: his prai - ses we'll sing!

34

UPPER VOICES: On Christ-mas night all Chris-tians sing, To hear the news the

S.A.: ___ we'll sing!_____ And when they were come, they their trea-sures un-

an - gels bring, On Christ-mas night all Chris-tians sing, To hear the news the an - gels bring— News of great

-fold,_ And un - to him of - fered myrrh, in - cense, and gold._ So bless - ed for

*Text and melody: Trad. English

joy, news of great mirth,_____ News of our mer - ci - ful_ King's
ev - er be Je - sus our King, Who brought us sal - va - tion: his prai - ses we'll

birth,_____ our mer - ci - ful_ King's birth._____ Re - joice!
sing,_____ his prai - ses we'll sing!_____ Re - joice!

Man.

Ped.

8. This is the Truth (II)

Trad. English

BOB CHILCOTT

*Melody by Henry John Gauntlett (1805–76); text by Mrs Cecil Frances Alexander (1818–95)

And he leads his chil-dren on To the place where he is gone.

if you want to know the way, Be pleased to hear what he did say.

mf

Man.

UPPER VOICES

p cresc.

God grant to all with-

S.

A.

p cresc.

Not in that poor, low-ly

T.

p cresc.

Not in that poor, low-ly sta-ble,

B.

p cresc.

Ped.

40

Processed in England by Enigma Music Production Services, Amersham, Bucks.
Printed in England by Halstan & Co. Ltd, Amersham, Bucks.